Debussy Masterpieces
for Solo Piano
20 Works

CLAUDE DEBUSSY

D1613773

DOVER PUBLICATIONS, INC.
Mineola, New York

Bibliographical Note

This Dover edition, first published in 2002, is a new compilation of twenty piano works originally published separately in authoritative early editions. The glossary is newly added. Some annotations in the main headings have been adapted from commentary in David Dubal's *The Art of the Piano* (Harcourt Brace & Company, New York, 1995).

International Standard Book Number: 0-486-42425-1

Manufactured in the United States of America
Dover Publications, Inc., 31 East 2nd Street, Mineola, N.Y. 11501

CONTENTS

Arabesque No. 1 (*1888–91*)   2

Clair de lune (*Moonlight, 1890–1905*)   22

Danse (*Dance, 1890*)   12

Des pas sur la neige (*Footprints in the snow, 1909–10*)   82

Feuilles mortes (*Dead leaves, 1912–13*)   96

Feux d'artifice (*Fireworks, 1912–13*)   110

Golliwogg's cakewalk (*1906–8*)   68

Jardins sous la pluie (*Gardens in the rain, 1903*)   28

Jimbo's lullaby (*1906–8*)   64

La cathédrale engloutie (*The engulfed cathedral, 1909–10*)   73

La fille aux cheveux de lin (*The girl with the flaxen hair, 1909–10*)   84

La plus que lente—Valse (*The "more than slow" waltz, 1910*)   90

La Puerta del Vino (*The Wine Gate, 1912–13*)   99

L'isle joyeuse (*The isle of joy, 1904*)   44

Minstrels (*1909–10*)   86

Ondine (*The water nymph Undine, 1912–13*)   103

Reflets dans l'eau (*Reflections in the water, 1905*)   57

Rêverie (*Revery, 1890*)   7

Soirée dans Granade (*Evening in Granada, 1903*)   38

Voiles (*Sails or Veils, 1909–10*)   78

GLOSSARY OF FRENCH TERMS

à l'aise, at ease

animez (un peu) (et augmentez peu à peu), becoming (a little more) lively (and gradually louder)

âpre, harsh

assez modéré, rather moderate

augmentez progressivement (sans presser), gradually louder (without rushing)

au Mouvement [Mouv^t] = *a tempo*

aussi léger que possible, as light as possible

avec de brusques oppositions d'extrême violence et de passionnée douceur [p. 99],
        with the sudden contrasts of extreme violence and impassioned tenderness

avec plus d'abandon, with greater abandon

avec une grande émotion, very emotionally

cédez (encore plus), slacken [*rallentando*] (even more)

ce rythme doit avoir la valeur sonore d'un fond de paysage triste et glacé [p. 82],
        this rhythmic passage should reflect the sound quality of a melancholy, frozen landscape

commencer lentement dans un rythme nonchalamment gracieux,
        begin slowly in a nonchalantly graceful rhythm

comme un echo de la phrase précédemment, like an echo of the preceding phrase

comme un tendre et triste regret, like a tender, sad regret

dans—in
        la sonorité du début, expressif et tendre, in the sonority of the opening, expressive and tender
        le sentiment du début, in the mood of the beginning
        une sonorité harmonieuse et lointaine, in a harmonious and distant sonority

*de plus en plus lent et **pp** jusqu'à la fin*, gradually slower and *pianissimo* until the end

de très loin, from a great distance

doucement— gently
        expressif, quietly expressive
        marqué, subtly accented
        soutenu et très expressif, gently sustained and very expressive

doux—soft, gentle
        et expressif, soft and expressive
        et harmonieux, soft and harmonious
        et un peu gauche, gentle and a bit awkward

éclatant, bursting forth

en animant (jusqu'à la fin) (surtout dans l'expression),
        becoming livelier (until the end) (especially in expression)

en augmentant beaucoup, become much louder

en cédant, slackening off (*rallentando*)

encore plus lent, even slower

en dehors, prominently, bring out [this passage]

en retenant (jusqu'à la fin), holding back (until the end)

en se calmant, calming down

en se rapprochant peu à peu = *accelerando poco a poco*

en serrant, speeding up (*stringendo*)

et plus gravement expressif, and more seriously expressive

et sans retarder, and without slowing down

expressif (et en dehors) (et concentré) (et douloureux),
               expressive (and emphasized) (and concentrated) (and mournfully)

flottant et sourd, floating and muffled

gracieux, graceful, gracious

incisif (et rapide), incisively (and quickly)

ironique, ironically

jusqu'à la fin, until the end

la ♩=♪ *de la mesure précédente* [p. 42] =
               the quarter note [of the present measure] equals the eighth note of the preceding measure

laissez vibrer, let ring

la m.g. en dehors, bring out the left hand

le double plus lent [This playing instruction from *Ondine*, p. 106, resembles the more common phrase
               plus lent du double, meaning "twice as slow."]

léger (egal et lointain) (et rythmé), light (even and distant) (and rhythmic)

lent et mélancolique, slow and melancholy

les basses légères et harmonieuses, the bass notes light and harmonious

les "gruppetti" sur le temps, [play] the grace notes on the beat

les 2 Ped., [depress] the two pedals

lointain, distant

marqué, accented, *marcato*

m.d. [M.D.] [main droit], right hand

m.g. [M.G.] [main gauche], left hand

modéré (et très souple) = *moderato* (and very flexible)

moins (rigoreux) (animé), less (rigorous) (animated)

moqueur, mockingly

mouvement = *tempo, a tempo*
         de Habanera, in the tempo of a Habanera
         du début = *Tempo I*
         élargi, in a broader tempo

murmuré et en retenant peu à peu, murmuring and *ritardando poco a poco*

mystérieux, mysterious

nerveux et avec humour, nervously and humorously

net et vif, distinct and lively

passionnément, passionately

peu à peu—little by little
         cresc. et animé, gradually louder and more animated
         sortant de la brume, gradually rising out of the mist

plus—more

> *à l'aise,* more easy-going
>
> *allant,* with more movement, *con moto*
>
> *animé,* more animated
>
> *lent,* slower

profondément calme (dans une brume doucement sonore),

> profoundly calm (in a gently sonorous mist)

rapide, quickly

retenu = *retenuto*

sans—without

> *lenteur,* without slowing down
>
> *lourdeur,* without heaviness
>
> *nuances,* without shading

scintillant, scintillating

sec (et retenu), dry (and *meno mosso*)

serrez, pressing (*stringendo*)

sonore sans dureté, sonorous without hardness

tempo animé, in a lively tempo

toujours retenu = *sempre retenuto*

très—very

> *calme et doucement expressif,* very calm and gently expressive
>
> *détaché,* very detached
>
> *doux (et très expressif),* very gentle (and very expressive)
>
> *en dehors,* very prominent
>
> *expressif,* very expressive
>
> *lent,* very slow
>
> *net et très sec,* very distinct and very dry
>
> *peu,* very little
>
> *retenu* = *molto retenuto*
>
> *rythmé,* very rhythmic

un peu—a little, somewhat

> *animé (jusqu'à la fin),* slightly animated (until the end)
>
> *au-dessous du mouvement,* at a somewhat slower tempo
>
> *cédé,* a little slower
>
> *en dehors,* a bit to the fore
>
> *moins lent (dans une expression allant grandissant),*
>
> > a little slower (with an increasingly great expressiveness)
>
> *moins vite,* not quite so fast
>
> *plus mouvementé (allant),* slightly quicker
>
> *retardé,* somewhat held back
>
> *retenu* = *poco retenuto*

DEBUSSY MASTERPIECES
for Solo Piano

Arabesque No. 1

From *Deux Arabesques* (1888–91)

Rêverie

Revery (1890)

Danse

Originally *Tarantelle styrienne* (1890);
republished as *Danse* (1903)

Clair de lune

Moonlight: Third of the four-part *Suite bergamasque*
(1890, revised 1905)

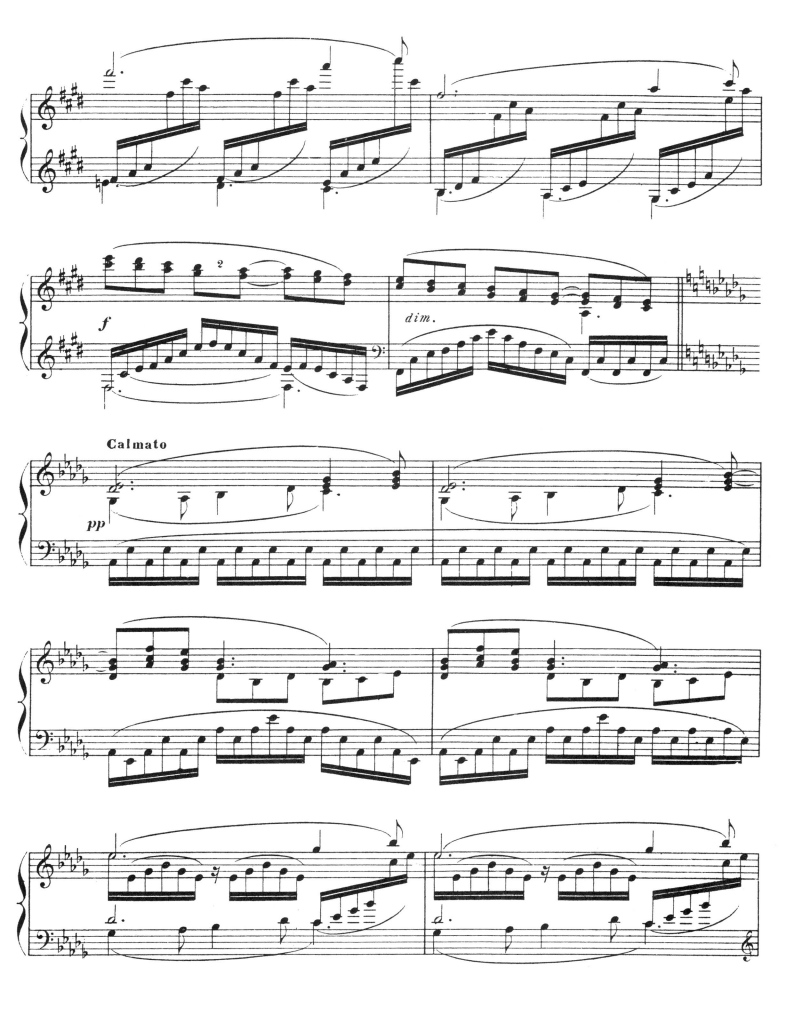

Jardins sous la pluie

Gardens in the rain: Last of the three-part
Estampes [Engravings] (1903)

Net et vif

Tempo – en animant jusqu'à la fin

Soirée dans Grenade

Evening in Granada: Second of the three-part
Estampes [Engravings] (1903)

Mouvement de Habanera
Commencer lentement dans un rythme nonchalamment gracieux

L'isle joyeuse

The isle of joy (1904), inspired by Antoine Watteau's painting
L'embarquement pour Cythère

Tempo: très animé jusqu'à la fin.

Reflets dans l'eau

Reflections in the water: First of the three-part
Images (First Series) (1905)

Andantino molto
(Tempo rubato)

1º Tempo (en retenant jusqu'à la fin)

sempre *pp*

Rit.

Lent (dans une sonorité harmo-

p un peu en dehors

nieuse et lointaine)

Jimbo's lullaby

Second of the six-part *Children's Corner* (1906–8)

Dedicated to his infant daughter, Claude-Emma ("Chou-Chou"); Jimbo was her toy elephant.

Golliwogg's Cakewalk

Last of the six-part *Children's Corner* (1906–8)

Golliwogg, a black male doll, was the gallant hero of popular children's books
written in the 1890s by Bertha Upton and illustrated by her daughter Florence Kate.

Allegro giusto

Un peu moins vite

La cathédrale engloutie

The engulfed cathedral: No. 10 of twelve *Preludes*, Book 1 (1909–10)

Based on the ancient Breton legend of the Cathedral of Ys, doomed for impiety, forever rising briefly from the sea each sunrise.

*) The direction ♩=♩ should appear over the barline between mm. 6 and 7; it should be canceled by the direction ♩=♩ over the barline between mm. 12 and 13. (This faster tempo in mm. 7–12, and later in mm. 22–83, can be heard on Debussy's piano-roll recording of this prelude.)

Peu à peu sortant de la brume

Augmentez progressivement (Sans presser)

Sonore sans dureté

*)The direction ♩=♩ should appear over the barline between mm. 83 and 84.

Voiles

Sails or *Veils*: No. 2 of twelve *Preludes*, Book 1 (1909–10)

Images of sailing boats and of "mysterious veils." Edgard Varèse believed the music
was inspired by the diaphonous veils used by American dancer Loïe Fuller, then famous in Paris.

Modéré (♪ = 88)

(Dans un rythme sans rigueur et caressant)

Des pas sur la neige

Footprints in the snow: No. 6 of twelve *Preludes*, Book 1 (1909–10)

Triste et lent (♩=44)

pp

piu pp

*Ce rythme doit avoir la valeur sonore
d'un fond de paysage triste et glacé.*

p expressif et douloureux

m.d.

pp

expressif

(2/4) Cédez   *retenu*

pp

pp

p

pp

La fille aux cheveux de lin

The girl with the flaxen hair: No. 8 of twelve *Preludes*, Book 1 (1909–10)

Inspired by a poem of Leconte de Lisle.

Minstrels

The last of twelve *Preludes*, Book 1 (1909–10)

Echoes of Parisian music halls and the American cakewalk.

La plus que lente–Valse

The "more than slow" waltz (1910)

Feuille mortes

Dead leaves: No. 2 of twelve *Preludes,* Book 2 (1912–13)

La Puerta del Vino

The Wine Gate: No. 3 of twelve *Preludes,* Book 2 (1912–13)

The famed "gateway to the vineyard" of Granada's Alhambra Palace

avec de brusques oppositions d'extrême
violence et de passionnée douceur

Ondine

The water nymph Undine: No. 8 of twelve *Preludes*, Book 2 (1912–13)

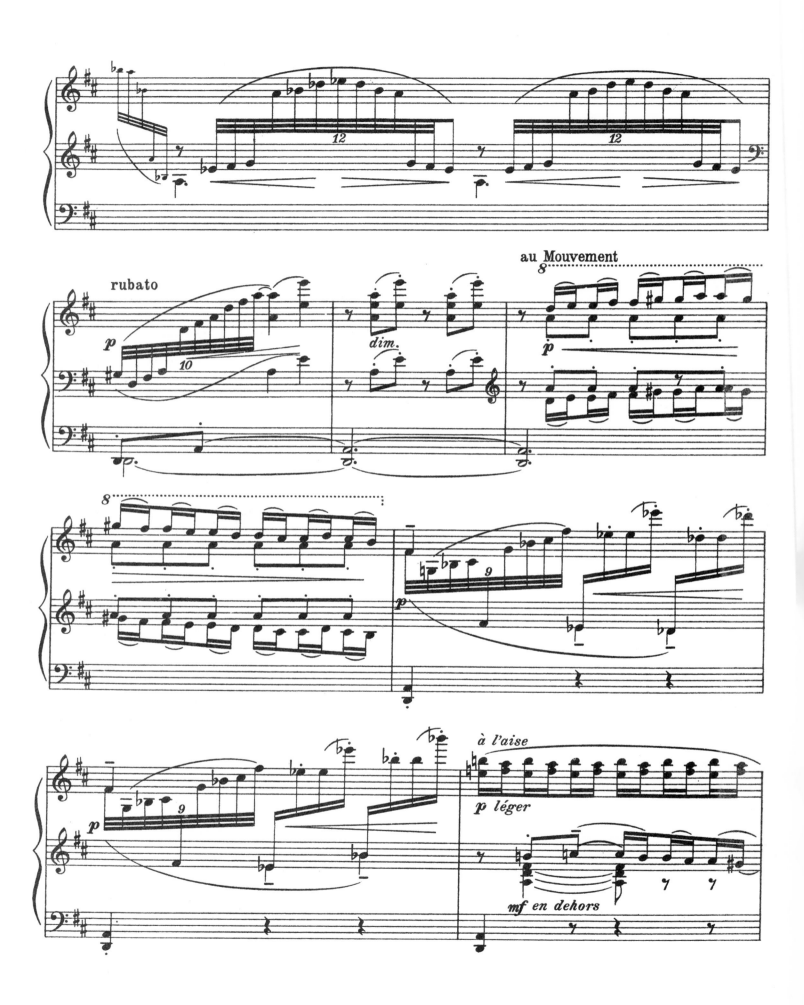

Feux d'artifice

Fireworks: The last of twelve *Preludes*, Book 2 (1912–13)

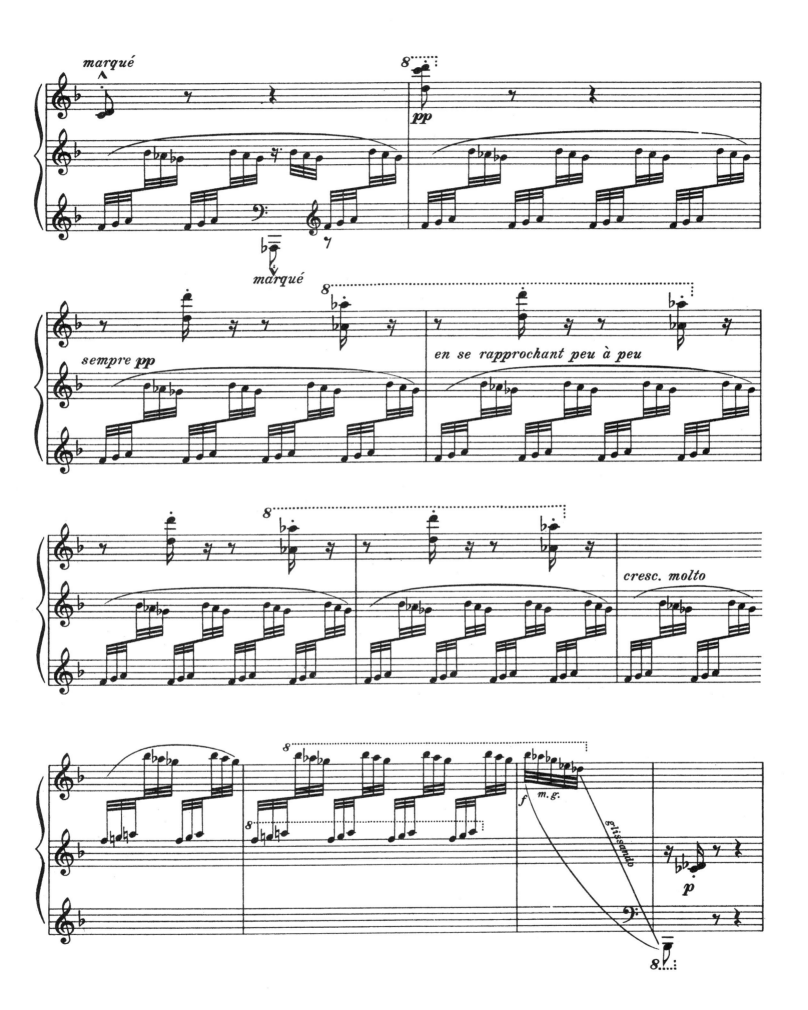

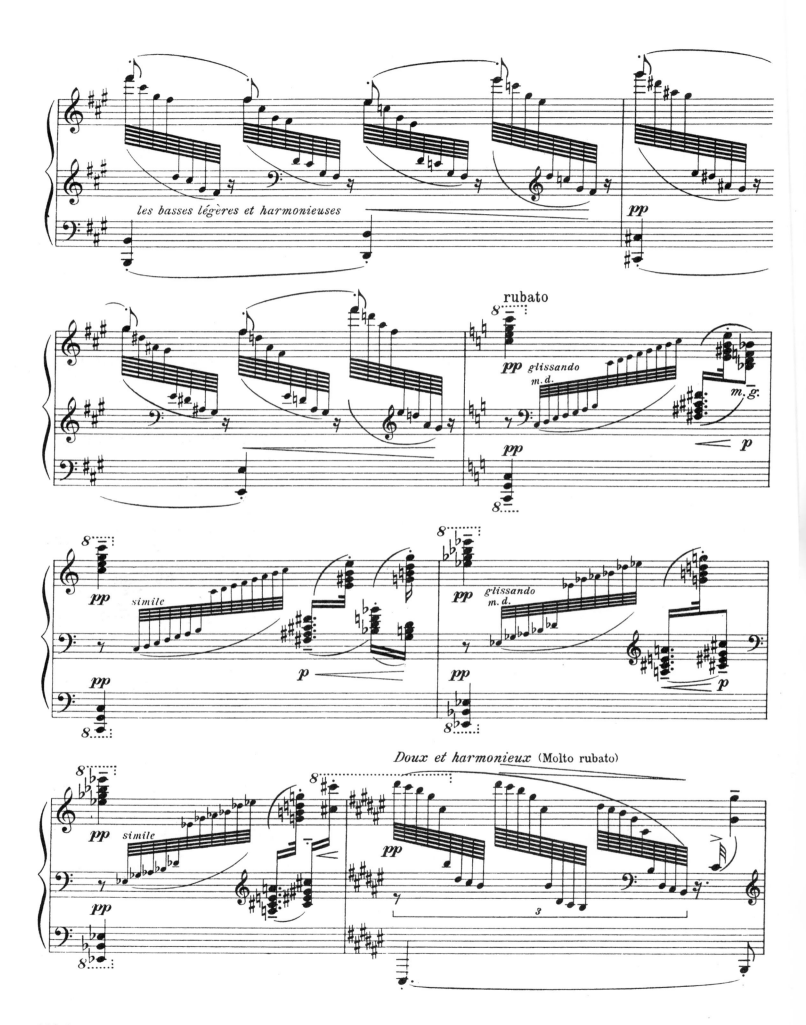